TWISTED

ALSO BY
CHARLOTTE CORBEIL-COLEMAN

Scratch

with Emily Sugerman:
The End of Pretending

ALSO BY
JOSEPH JOMO PIERRE

Beatdown: Three Plays
Shakespeare's Nigga

TWISTED

BY CHARLOTTE CORBEIL-COLEMAN
AND JOSEPH JOMO PIERRE

PLAYWRIGHTS CANADA PRESS
TORONTO

For professional or amateur production rights, please contact:
The Gary Goddard Agency
149 Church Street, 2nd Floor
Toronto, ON M5B 1Y4
416.928.0299, www.garygoddardagency.com/apply-for-performance-rights/

LIBRARY AND ARCHIVES CANADA CATALOGUING IN PUBLICATION
Corbeil-Coleman, Charlotte, author

    Twisted / Charlotte Corbeil-Coleman and Joseph Jomo Pierre. -- First edition.

Issued in print and electronic formats.
ISBN 978-1-77091-762-0 (softcover).--ISBN 978-1-77091-763-7 (PDF).--ISBN 978-1-77091-764-4 (HTML).--ISBN 978-1-77091-765-1 (Kindle)

    I. Pierre, Joseph Jomo, 1975-, author II. Title.

PS8555.O595T85 2017   C812'.6   C2017-901355-6
                                                       C2017-901356-4

We acknowledge the financial support of the Canada Council for the Arts, the Ontario Arts Council (OAC), the Ontario Media Development Corporation, and the Government of Canada through the Canada Book Fund for our publishing activities.

Charlotte

To my fearless leader, who knew real magic lived in words.
Thank you for bringing Joseph Jomo Pierre into my life
and work. I love you, Iris Turcott.
—Scarlett

Joseph

Iris Turcott. This play would not have been made without
her guiding hands. A true lover of the WORD. She made
my life fuller, my convictions entrenched.
As she championed my words,
I champion her intellect, boldness, and spirit.
I love you, Iris.
—Dew Hickey

To my partner in crime, Charlotte Corbeil-Coleman—
having our words dance together was a blessing.

I would also like to thank my family for their continued
support. Tyrus, Amiri, Naliyah, and of course my love,
Sarah, the embodiment of goodness. Love you all.

FOREWORD

Below is an excerpt from a letter of support Iris Turcott wrote for Joseph Jomo Pierre and Charlotte Corbeil-Coleman's Factory Theatre residency.

I want to give you a brief account of how this project came into being. Charlotte and I were discussing adaptation possibilities when we had a kind of EUREKA moment when we hit on Dickens's *Oliver Twist*. It became immediately clear that the original narrative was so sadly relevant and compelling, that little needed to be changed except the historical context. Also, this was the first novel that was child-centric and Dickens used his protagonist to heighten the impact of his astute and scathing social commentary about the world in which he lived. The world in which we live is still plagued by some of the same systemic injustices and inequities, but there are also a whole new set of social and political challenges to contend with and our technological culture is both a curse and a blessing in terms of addressing them. This sometimes dehumanizing culture of technology will be central to how this adaptation is realized theatrically.

Originally Charlotte envisioned this as a one-man/boy play and we both knew it could only be Joseph Pierre—not just because Joe was the perfect actor for the piece but because Charlotte imagined her modern-day Oliver becoming a spoken-word/rap performer and those "pieces" would have to be created and delivered authentically. Joe's hard-hitting rhythms and muscular poetics are a perfect counterpoint to Charlotte's quirky and delicious female cadences.

But a funny thing happened on the way to *Twisted*. Charlotte and Joe decided mutually to focus in on the Nancy/Oliver relationship as a way to theatrically compress this epic. Another EUREKA moment—they quickly hit on the idea that this was a two-hander where Charlotte would write Nancy and Joe would write Oliver. The story would emerge through a series of their individual monologues—phone, text, and email contact—with probably one real direct scene with the two of them.

Finally, these are two of the most gifted and provocative young writers on the national scene today, but in combination they are even more electric. They are both uncompromising, opinionated, and driven by their relentless pursuit of artistic excellence, and I know sparks will fly when they begin collaborating. It is also completely fitting that the process of creation (a Black male writer collaborating with a white female writer while maintaining their own singular voices) so reflects the form of this brave, unique adaptation of this strangely relevant classic.

Iris Turcott
Dramaturge

Iris Turcott was a dramaturge, director, and actor. She was also co-founder and co-artistic director of Playbill Theatre. She was the company dramaturge at the Canadian Stage Company and Factory Theatre, working with playwrights from coast to coast, including Adam Pettle, Joan MacLeod, Michel Marc Bouchard, Brad Fraser, Judith Thompson, Robert Chafe, Ronnie Burkett, Anusree Roy, and Tomson Highway. She passed away in September 2016.

Twisted was first produced by Factory Theatre and b current at the Factory Theatre Mainspace, Toronto, between January 31 to February 22, 2015. It featured the following cast and creative team:

Nancy: Susanna Fournier
Oliver: Ngabo Nabea

Directed by Nigel Shawn Williams
Set designed by Denyse Karn
Composed by Hagler
Lighting designed by Simon Rossiter
Projections/video designed by Simeon Taole
Sound designed by Richard Lee
Costumes designed by Michelle Bailey

CHARACTERS

Oliver: Black (biracial), seventeen years old, fostered.

Nancy: White, twenty-three years old, sex-trade worker.

CHARACTERS THAT ARE MENTIONED

Sikes: White, runs a sex ring.

Dodger: White, Sikes's right-hand man.

Big Bird: White, Oliver's last foster parent.

Rose: Black (biracial), twelve.

NOTE

In the original production all text messages were displayed as projections.

In black.

NANCY
He called me Lady Porcelain. Ollie gives everyone names; he says it helps life become a story, so that then when it ends bad you can close the book on it.

Nancy

Surprises like misfortunes seldom come alone.

Lights follow OLIVER. *It's early, early morning and still dark out so it's hard to make out exactly where he is. All we feel is concrete on concrete.*

OLIVER
She's just watching back.
Rough edges and all,
How real is that.
It keeps coming back.

Memories
Keep coming back.
Sometimes in pencil,
Sometimes in ink.
Sometimes it's stencilled.
Dem times I think,
How real is that.

Ain't doing no justice,
If there ain't no real in that.
One a.m.
No alarm,
Keep waking up.
Two a.m.
No one around,
Just speaking out loud tryna make up.

He looks out to the audience.

Two things you should know before we really begin.

A dim light like the faint glow of a laptop comes up on
NANCY.

NANCY
So far there are three things that I know to be absolutely true of life.

OLIVER
I'm seventeen.

NANCY
Toothbrushes only last three months.

OLIVER
I have a morbid fear of hot dogs. They're not my worst fear, but they scare me. Deeply.

NANCY
It's your first love that creates you and your second love that changes you.

OLIVER
I can't tell you my worst fear yet. I will. But it takes time.
Explaining.

NANCY
Every rose has a thorn.

OLIVER
. . . One more thing you should know.

NANCY
One more thing—

OLIVER
I've been running since I was born.

NANCY
No one gets to say goodbye.

> *NANCY watches OLIVER, but he does not see her. He's turned
> away from her presence, stuck looking down at his phone.*

Nancy

Women can always put things in fewest words.

> *OLIVER begins to scroll through his phone.*

OLIVER
When even your bones can feel it. How real is that?

> *A light comes up on NANCY. The light is tight around her
> face and body, making it impossible to see the rest of the
> space she exists in.*

Except when it's blowing up and then they lengthen it out.

NANCY moves slowly towards the audience and smiles mysteriously.

NANCY
I believe in magic and I hate blueberries.
I was eight years old playing at a park. It was one of those old parks, you know with wood and nails—a park you could fucking die in.

Not like now where everything is shapeless and plastic. Dummy-proof.

That's why kids are fat now.

I see them in these bubble-boy parks, just waddling into things. We had to be nimble, or you'd lose an eye.

Fear keeps you in shape.

It was cold out, not freezing, but I remember wearing the wrong jacket. I was always wearing the wrong jacket.

A season behind.

I'd get my winter coat in spring and be boiling but feel like I had to wear it 'cause I had been so goddamned cold all winter in a windbreaker.

Hand-me-downs.

Yeah my childhood was one big hand-me-down.

As soon as I was making my own money, the first thing I bought: this big bubble jacket. Yeah, white. So you can see all the stains of life and then wash them off. Bought it at Joe Fresh. Because I like his name. In fact I'd like to marry Joe. Nancy Fresh has a nice ring to it, don't you think?

When I'm cold, I go into a deep, stay-in-bed, drink–a–bottle–of–Jack Daniel's, see-you-later depression.

> OLIVER *remains focused on his phone. Scrolling through, he stops on a text.*

Nancy

> **Dignity and holiness are often more questions of coat and waistcoat than people imagine.**

OLIVER
I'd dress all the angels in white/bubble/wrap.

NANCY
So, I'm playing in the kind of park that could kill you if you went down the slide the wrong way and it's see-your-breath kind of cold and I'm pretending I'm smoking 'cause I think it's funny. I roll up these little pieces of paper and just breathe out.

> *She pretends to do it.*

so this group of blondeblonde girls—that's how I remember them, blondeblonde—I hate blondes. They come up to me and say, "Hey do you believe in maaaaaagic."

They say, "Try licking the pole. It taaaastes like blueberries!"

I was pretty sure they were full of shit, but there was this little feeling, deep in my belly, the maybe-magic-*is-real* feeling.

She shakes her head.

so, I opened my mouth and stuck out my tongue . . .

I was stuck to that fucking pole for three hours.

Almost lost my tongue. Had to go to the hospital.

My mom was pissed 'cause it made her look bad. And now when I see a blueberry I want to punch someone in the face.

She looks at OLIVER *longingly but he remains focused on his phone.*

But I still believe in magic.

Nancy

What games did you play as a child?

OLIVER stares at his phone.

Oliver

More like run into the woods.

OLIVER
Told her I was jealous of that pole
That was stuck to her lips.
She said I was stupid.
"You're so stupid."
But then she hit me up with a Snapchat
With a close-up,

Of her lips.
The only way that we kiss.
All you heard is,
Stupid.
But I heard,
From her tone,
That unsaid verb,
That was so hard for her to say.
"Elephant shoe."
Don't say it, just mouth it.

He mouths it as NANCY speaks it.

NANCY
Elephant shoe.

OLIVER
My return was unrehearsed,
But sprung from a youthful place.
"Olive juice."
Don't say it, just mouth it.
Started with word games,
But slowly,
Talking 'bout hurtful things.
And slowly,
Quickly falling
For
What it is
Humans be looking for.

Nancy

If this were a tale of unmixed joy and happiness,
it would be very brief.

OLIVER looks down at his phone.

I'd rather see you smile one time than to see you frown one hundred times. Lies. I'd rather see you.

NANCY
You ever hear phantom rings? I get them all the time.

Like the ghosts of cellphones past.

I could divide my life into before and after. Before I had a cell and after.

Before I had a cellphone I was never in touch. I don't buy any of this "technology has brought us so far apart" bullshit. Nothing says love to me like the buzz/bing/bang of getting a text.

All I need is my jacket and my cell. I'm good to go.

People think you are closer to someone face to face; people think true intimacy is touching someone. Well let me tell you, I've been face in face with a lot of people, I've held on to a lot of backs, and there ain't nothing close about it.

I get a text, I feel close inside.

Nancy
tell me three things you see everyday.

Oliver
Sidewalks. Nooks. Pain.

You?

Wrist. Chest. Thigh.

We both got scars—hell, you could play connect the dots with mine. Difference is his came before and mine came after.

NANCY speaks her text aloud:

Nancy

If you could forget one thing what would it be?

OLIVER continues to scroll through his texts.

Oliver

The picking of scabs.

Ollie's got one big scar on his stomach. The boyfriend of his first foster mom came home drunk, took his steel-toed shoe, and went off on him. Beat him unconscious and put him in the closet. Paramedics had no idea how long he was out.

He had four broken ribs and thirteen stitches on his belly.

This rib, this one *(touches it)*—has been broken three times. This one here—it keeps rebreaking.

Breaking a rib is like having a bird dying slowly in your chest.

OLIVER moves, agitated. NANCY watches him. She speaks her text aloud:

Nancy

What does love smell like?

OLIVER relaxes a little.

Cigarettes and chlorine.

It's your first love that creates you and your second love that changes you. Cigarettes and chlorine is the smell of Ollie's first love.

She takes a deep breath, touching her rib delicately.

This woman that was taking care of him, his "foster mom" with the drunk boyfriend, had a daughter. She was sixteen.

She took Ollie to the pool every Sunday in the summer; she would smoke behind the fence. She bought him McDonald's when he got hungry. He'd eat McNuggets and she'd suck out the ketchup from those plastic packages.

She wore miniskirts and tights that were too small for her so she waddled.

She took him everywhere, holding his hand even when it got sweaty. They slept in the same bed.

He loved her. Then one night she said she had to go out and he couldn't come; she said she wasn't his girlfriend and she wasn't his mother and she left.

Nancy

It opens the lungs, exercises the eyes, and softens down the temper. So cry away.

He cried all night. That's what sent the boyfriend off. The sound of Ollie crying. That's why he got beat up and ended up in hospital. After the stitches came out he couldn't stop picking at the scab, so it never healed proper and left him with a wicked scar.

And he never cried again—lives running from those tears.

Ollie got sent from that foster home to three others until he got to Big Bird. That's what you called her. Big Bird. Ollie gives everyone names; it helps make life a story so that then when it ends bad . . .

She looks at him pleadingly. He doesn't see her but looks away from the sense of her. He focuses on reading more texts.

Big Bird was different than the rest. She was a tall blonde woman with a nice home. She was lonely but she was nice. She cared about you.

She put candles in the bathroom and he had his own bedroom. She was prepared to go all out for him.

Everything was going okay until he turned thirteen. She had a party for him with those funny triangle hats and an ice cream cake with a big truck on it.

So all these kids from school came and Big Bird made hot dogs and there were balloons . . . He said he'd never seen a balloon before . . . funny what you can miss in the system. Or just life. I never knew you were supposed to spit out toothpaste, no one ever taught me that. Sikes—

Both NANCY and OLIVER react with their bodies to the word Sikes.

—was like, "Shit, girl, that's disgusting—not that." He taught me what to swallow.

So everything is perfect and the kids play a game, let's pretend it was pin the tail on a donkey 'cause that game cracks me up, all these blind children trying to get a tail on the ass of a donkey. And then they sit down to eat the hot dogs, but in all this perfect preparation, in all the getting the cake and blowing up balloons, Big Bird forgot to cook the hot dogs.

So Oliver bites into a cold, raw wiener.

He got really silent and then left. Thirteen.

Ran as fast as he could.

That's when I knew I loved him.

When I heard that story.

He had the perfect childhood handed to him and it ended with a cold wiener.

Nancy
Mustard, Ketchup, or Relish?

Oliver
Ketchup.

OLIVER
She asked me to blink,
So she could enter my mind.
Thousand questions that caused me,
To slow down time.
She's flicking through my past,
For pieces to mine.
Nance, it's too dark, too dark.
There's nothing to find.
But she's freeze-framing,
And rearranging,

Charlotte Corbeil-Coleman & Joseph Jomo Pierre

Layering and stitching,
Quilting,
Pieces of me.

And wrapping herself in it.
And finding warmth in it.
She's made her map and key.

NANCY speaks her text aloud:

Nancy

**What do you think about before you close
your eyes?**

Oliver

I think of beginnings.

NANCY speaks her text aloud:

Nancy

If you could go anywhere, where would it be?

Oliver

How far is far away and could we visit someday.

OLIVER
How far is far away . . .

NANCY
I remember I found a map online for this stupid kids' maze in
Niagara. At the end of the maze there was a picture of a family
with their eyes and mouths wide open. Like this.

She does an expression of exaggerated mock surprise.

I was obsessed with it—all I wanted was to go to Niagara.

I had no interest in the actual falls.

Fuck them.

I think anyone who sees something that huge just wants to jump.

The best part is everything else. I wanted the wax house and gumballs. I wanted simulated coaster rides and old people jerking off slot machines. I wanted haunted houses with signs that clearly blink EXIT.

That's the incredible thing about Niagara Falls, there's all these fake things around it. All competing. All trying to dazzle and failing. Just like us humans. We're just the crap around everything else that belongs here.

Nancy
What's the first touch you remember?

Oliver
Stiff Sheets.

Ollie went through the WHOLE system. Fosters. Street. Shelter. *Then* Dodger.

Me? I went through Boredom.

Nancy
What's the first taste you remember?

Oliver
Something bitter. My mom musta had bad book milk.

*Boob milk.

My mom would get me to play hide-and-go-seek—it was her favourite game—problem was, she'd never come find me . . .

Nancy

Tell me three things about your mother.

Oliver

You should stop. This is stupid. Rather talk about the shape of shit.

What do you think she looked like?

No time for this white mama crap.

NANCY speaks her text aloud:

Nancy

You want me. you gotta give me you.

OLIVER takes this in. He looks at his response on his phone. Speaking it out loud as it appears as a series of long texts he once sent. He gets caught up in the reading of it.

Oliver

White mama, Black daddy, White mama,
Black me.
Why she take the nut, if she ain't want the seed?
Why she ain't see a doctor,
30 days no bleed?
Why she ain't take the white pill,
If she ain't want me?
Plan "B"
Shoulda take the white pill would never love me.
White mama, White mama.

Is it true, what they say about you mama?
Too poor for the white man to wife you mama.
Ass too fat so they spite you mama.
Same ass make a migrant take delight in
you mama.
So you took your plight to where white was right
and he bagged you mama.
Pick apples, pick grapes, pick your cherry.
White drama.

There she go that,
Trailer trash.
Smoking weed, listening to rap.
White drama.
There she go that,
Queen of spades,
B.B.W.
Loving B.B.C.
White drama.

There she go just,
Sitting on her ass,
Watching Maury,
Collecting pogey.
Drama.

Make you kill a Mocking bird.

Pause.

Mama
I'm just tryna fill in the blanks
That your truancy left.

With mocking words chirped out
With hatred's breath.
On the playgrounds, sidewalks,
And from caregiver's chest.
This is the mess,
Absentee love left.
This is the nightly weight,
That balloons my head.

Maybe, none of it is true.
Maybe, you were young and scared.
Maybe, it's an injustice,
That maybes can't slay demons,
Or spook them out of heads.
White mama, white mama, white mama,
Black anx/i/e/ties.

NANCY stares at him, taking him in fully. She speaks aloud the text she once sent him.

Nancy

Hey, I see you. Welcome. Come on in, to me.

I knew early on I had to find a map out of me.

I grew up in Verona, Ontario.

Yup, fair Verona. Ha. A stop-in from the highway—but a stop-in with no Timmy Ho's—so not really a stop-in at all.

Mostly car lots and unhappy women. Years of giving sad blow jobs and getting bad dye jobs makes you go CRAZY.

People think it's rough in the city but no one knows what happens in the cunt of small town Ontario.

My mom believed she could turn off things with her mind . . . She'd sit in front of the TV looking for spirits that lived between the channels. In the fuzz. I blame TV—there are too many shows about special people. My dad drove three hours to work and three hours home, though a lot of the time he stayed over in Toronto. You know the story—crazy mom/commuting dad.

I didn't envy them—that family at the end of the maze with the *(she does the impression of their expression again)* I only wondered what it would be like to have a family that could all have the exact same expression of surprise.

There are a lot of different ways we become orphans.

Oliver

I feel you, like a lip real close to a neck.

Nancy

I hear you, like an ear pressed against a beating chest.

Fingers intertwined. Thumbs mutually stroking. Is this where we're at?

Yes. Hand in hand, then hands to face, tracing. What is my outline?

Doesn't matter, cause we're going deeper and deeper and deeper . . .

Straight to colouring each other in.

yeh. but then it gets dirty right lol.

NANCY laughs, a wonderful childlike laugh. It changes, echoes, repeats. OLIVER reacts with the sharpness of the memory.

Nancy

hahahaha send me a picture 😏

Oliver

You nuh ready yet lol.

NANCY hiccups. She is disoriented.

I'd do anything for you.

Tell the story of when we first met.

OLIVER shifts. He scrolls through more texts.

He pauses. She looks at him. OLIVER feels her look on his body but does not turn to her.

Please.

OLIVER looks down, pained. NANCY, impatient, takes charge.

. . . It was the afternoon and I was annoyed. Dodger was late with my package. I had been waiting so long there was a hand in my chest coming out.

NANCY looks at OLIVER. She continues.

Dodger is Sikes's second. He gets the boys into the brotherhood. They deal in movement—a different kind than us.

NANCY steps towards OLIVER.

Dodger had never sent someone else to me. I couldn't figure out why he did it. He was my get guy and he loved lording it over me, but this one day he stayed in the car.

Dodger had—

She waits for OLIVER *to speak.*

Ollie! Dodger had—

OLIVER
White boy had a smile on his face painted with trouble;
Or maybe it was more devious in nature.
You know
When the bottom lip is licked and the top licked after.
And the neck seems to pivot
Side to side in an effortless manner.
That's my dude right there.
Dodger at the fullest.
Something up the sleeve.
Dodger at the fullest.
All I got was a,

"Grab this, let's roll,"

As he flung me the keys.
Seventeen.

You know I ain't got no driver's licence.
And after dark I can't front and say I was just practisin.

"Grab this, let's roll"—slight-ly ir-ri-ta-ted at the re-peat-in.

Look, *man*, I look like shit, *man*, and youse all dappered up with
a fresh pair of jeans *and* them kicks you gave the toothbrush treat-
ment yesterday, *man*. And I swear you done popped three of them
Listerine strips *in* your mouth. And you just rolled up—just a
minute ago, *man*.

Pause.

"Ha ha ha ha ha," he started gassing.
"Ha ha ha ha ha, you got hella street for a country bumpkin.
Just chill, just chill, just chill nah man.
Just chill nah man.
Just chill nah man.
You always in that boxing stance,
Front hand guarding your face,
Ready for the block and counterpunch.
Just chill nah man.
You rolling with me now.
You flying under my wing.
Take the keys, jump the gas
I have to run a little deal."

I know that didn't make me eighteen
In an instant
And it didn't make my / purrmit a licence.
But I was under his wing,
And somehow that meant something.
We made a couple of lefts,
And a couple of rights,
But somehow it felt like I'd been driving all night.
Somehow my apprehension was lost to the night.
Young boy,
Composed,
Behind the wheel.

So relaxed that only my right hand did the driving.
Left hand on the door panel taking a nap.

What's her name? I know a chick's involved.
C'mon, Dodger. What's her name?

"The caged bird."

> *He can't continue. He's too emotional.* NANCY *stands up and moves into a new place on the stage. A middle ground between them. The lights are dim but warm. She speaks softly.*

NANCY
Hey.

> OLIVER *doesn't see her but he hears her.*

OLIVER
"The caged bird
Is a homegirl of mine.
If she shit or piss
Her man wanna know the time.
Prick like that.
Dude's mad protective.
After the skin show,
Back in her cage.
After the rub and tug,
Back in her cage.
Dude ain't got no scruples.
For the right amount of cash
He'd have her give that ass up
Right in her cage."

Beat.

"So every then and now
I drop her off a little masking tape
Her way to deal with the drain."

Ohh shit, how old is she?

"Twenty-three."

Twenty-three?

The number just sat in the air.

"Foot off the gas
It's that building right there.
Them dudes playing dice
Right there.
Okay, good timing.
She always on the second hand.
It's nine o'clock
She should be right—"

Pause.

"—here."

I never woulda believed
That someone could be so precise,
But she was.
I figured a worn-out chick
Who'd had enough.
Emaciated, cracked out,
Skinny-ass legs

Thighs been beated out.
Cigarette toothbrush,
Teeth nicotined out.

Pause.

I figured, but my numbers were wrong.
If you never heard the preface
You never woulda known.
She was thick in all the places
Dudes always brag they want.
She had those hook-er boots
But/her/walk
Was much different.
And if lips are indicative
Her talk would be much different.

Pause.

"Ha ha ha ha," Dodger started gassing.
"Now ain't you glad you came?"

NANCY
First time I met Ollie he gave me the hiccups. It was a butterfly massacre.

OLIVER
Contraband in hand,
Left Dodger in the car.

She was,
Pulling on those no-name cigasticks,
When
The scent met my reservation.

Lips puckered, then spit it out,
As her finger flipped it about.
Dexterity of a rhythmic gymnast,
Tobacco baton teasing her mouth.

How much mirror time it took,
To get this routine mastered?
For it was well mastered
And
Mastered for a while.

No
Burnt freckles present between her fingers.
No
Ash traces on her knuckles.

Though she said nothing,
Her non-verbal was loud.
It said
She was comfy in her skin,
This is who she was.
And
Yeh I look good,
And youse wishing you could touch.

Hell yeah she looked good.
I was wishing I could touch,
Wishing I could claim,
Wishing I could white Nike,
And
Name pendant gold chain.

But I remember what Dodger had said.
Went back to that refrain.

Somewhere behind this self-assuredness
There had to be some pain.

But I couldn't see no cracks
In my Lady Porcelain.

It was obvious she wasn't 'bout,
Putting it out for all to see.
Obvious she had no care
For shared sympathies
And fake niceties.
Couldn't blame her for it
I felt that way myself.

NANCY

First thing I noticed: he was my size. And he walked like he was
a guest on the earth. Not like Sikes, who walks like the ground
is his bitch.

I looked right at him but I couldn't breathe.

>   *She closes her eyes.*

Pin me.

>   *OLIVER sees NANCY in his memory. Her eyes still closed. She
>   opens them with force and they stare at each other, the warm
>   lights holding them. OLIVER approaches NANCY.*

OLIVER

(smiles) Look at this, we bonding
And haven't shared a word.
I'm just looking at this phoenix,

Thinking
How it's a caged bird.

And she's watching this dude
Stepping to her side.
Not much of a step,
Really more like a glide.

Who knows what kinda dissecting
She's doing of my insides.

NANCY
Where's Dodger?

OLIVER
Keep your head up,
Don't look to the ground.

You're in good hands.

NANCY
Really.

OLIVER
Don't use the simp card,
It never gets the chick.
Buys a lot of shit
But it never gets the chick.

You already know,
Did your deducing
From the time I opened the door.

NANCY
If you say so. Do you have something for me?

OLIVER
Look,
I let the first interrogation slide
But how you gonna do that,
Not even a hi.
What I look like
Your personal UPS guy.

NANCY
Hello.

OLIVER
That's better than hi.

Then she gave the hint of a smirk
Crept from down inside.
But her constitution
Wouldn't allow this display.

NANCY
I could feel them coming. Belly to chest. The air kept tightening in my esophagus.
Pin me.

OLIVER
So she
Dipped in her back pocket
And pulled out her phone.
Scrolled through the menu,
Hoping I'd leave well alone.

NANCY
Like when you swing so high you can feel gravity in your crotch.
Pin me.

I have to get back up, you gonna give that to me?

OLIVER
Should I touch it?
Should I leave it alone?

She knows that you seen it,
Just leave it alone.

So I reached out,
Put my fingers on her phone.
Her hand wasn't heavy
So she was easily disarmed.
And she wasn't saying nothing,
Just standing her ground.

> *NANCY's fingers touch his. Everything stops for a moment with their touch.*

NANCY
Like smoking a cigarette before you're awake.
Pin me.

OLIVER
Found her contact list
Put down what I had to put down.

Here, that's my pin.
And I gave her back her phone.

Then she did the reaching
And I was disarmed.
She took the baggy
Turned her back
And was gone.

NANCY walks away back to her space.

Her bandwidth on words
Musta been exceeded for the day.
Not even a goodbye
She just simply walked away.
But the back
Of those thighs
Said all she had to say.

NANCY
Pin me.

Hiccup.

This was all that came out. A hurricane of hiccups. Drove Sikes
nuts, nothing hot about—

She hiccups.

They lasted five hours until I got my first text from you.

She looks at OLIVER longingly.

It said . . .

OLIVER brings his phone to his chest and speaks into it.

Text appears as OLIVER *speaks:*

HEY

NANCY *looks at him as she holds up her package of pills (OxyContin); he raises his phone to his lips and takes a deep breath in.*

NANCY
Every Rose has a thorn.

OLIVER
I should stop here.

NANCY
I'm the girl who's stuck. You're the boy who's afraid.

OLIVER
No, no, I have to stop here.

He drops the phone. She takes off her jacket.

The lights change abruptly. OLIVER *is frozen.* NANCY *changes.*

NANCY *dumps the contents of her purse out on the floor.*

NANCY
How'd we get here? Here. How'd I get here? That's always the question, isn't it? How? How come? How'd she become this?

But that's so boring. Isn't it?

You know the story. You do. Girl fucks. Girl gets fucked over.

I'm already bored of this.

Girl is lonely in Ontario. She goes online. She meets a man called Sikes. He likes her profile pic; she likes his company.

Girl comes to city. To a group home. Sikes finds her. He doesn't need to try too hard. Works her in hard. She opens up. She's less bored. She learns why things sting. She's elastic. She's good with words. She lives on her computer, looking at maps to other things. She brings girls in. Who cares? She doesn't. White pill. Yum. These are the important things. All the other words are just fancy. Fancy Nancy.

She laughs.

The girls go into horrible houses with one white wall.

The newspapers call them Trick Pads. Used to be motels. But the city is expanding. A bawdy house. A place to go. And you know what? It actually looks a lot like TV.

His ladies are fourteen but sometimes younger. Hard to get the real young ones on the screen. He doesn't touch the young ones. He runs a business. But he gives them drugs, so he touches their brain. They get a TV. They sit and watch *Judge Judy*. They like when she gets mad.

I like when she gets mad.

At the beginning you get a twenty-dollar nail job. Maybe an outfit from Forever 21. They have some cute things. Hope you like sparkles. They're cheap as fuck.

You know the story. I thought I did too . . . Until I met Rose.

OLIVER's phone rings from the ground. He doesn't move.

Come on.

The phone continues to ring. He stands, stuck.

Come on. COME ON!

It gets louder and louder and louder, until the phone becomes earth-shatteringly loud.

NANCY looks at OLIVER, her eyes piercing him.

Ollie!

OLIVER picks up his phone.

The world of the play changes. NANCY is now trapped in a room with a laptop and a white wall.

OLIVER is in the streets.

Hundreds of texts fly by. Their whole relationship through texts appears.

We are now in a form of real time as OLIVER relives what actually happened.

Hey.

OLIVER

. . .

NANCY

I need your help.

OLIVER

Yeah, you need me when you need to kill time or some fuckin ox. Needle and thread don't always mend.

NANCY

Please. This is real. Ollie, please, just listen. / Listen to me.

OLIVER

Ask your man.

NANCY

I can't. Sikes is gonna . . . I can't turn this one. I can't turn her. This is really bad . . . I can't do this anymore. Sikes can't have this one. This girl's not for sale. I can't do it. I can't do this.

Beat.

I have to get out.

OLIVER

You said you could never leave him, now it's over???

NANCY

This time it's different. Please, you have to believe me. You have to. This girl needs us. She looks like . . .

Silence.

You know you have me.

OLIVER
No I don't.

NANCY
I'm yours.

OLIVER
I gotta go—

NANCY
Do this one thing for me, pick her up and we leave.

Beat. He hangs up on her. NANCY *holds the phone to her chest.*

OLIVER
Thought I opened up walls,
Expanded the perimeter.
Wonderland, girl in hand,
Rabbit hole out.

But now her dreams,
Are becoming my nightmare.
And my dreams,
Seem fictional,
White Hare.

She putting up walls,
Tryna encase me in this shit.
Bedpan full of piss,
Baptize me in this shit.

(Relax)
(You angry)

Can't reconcile,
Pimp hand over me?
Yeh I'm the one she chats to,
But he's the one she see.
I get lol smiley face,
He gets her garden,
Spade and rake.

(Relax)
Maybe,
I've exceeded,
This unwelcoming stay,
And what I need to do is,
Push, push, skate
And be on my way.

Nancy

Her name is Rose. We have to save her.

NANCY
I met her at the Eaton Centre. By A&W. She was picking nail polish off her thumb. I like to buy them a root beer 'cause the sugar gets 'em giddy.
She said: "Hi, my name is Rose. What's your name?"

Life is all about rules. The rules you make, the rules you break, and the rules that are made for you.

Sikes's rule: Bribe 'em. Flatter 'em. Feed 'em. Teach 'em. Dope 'em. Give them over.

Ollie's rule: name them as soon as I see them. Never say their real name out loud.

She smiled at me. She was young—but hell, I've seen younger. She had curly thick brown hair and a big gap in between her front teeth. Stunning. Small. Sad. I had no idea what to call her.

I said, "What's your favourite colour?"

She said "purple."

I hate purple.

I said, "We're going shopping."

"Goodie."

Goodie.

I said, "We should get you a nice dress."

She said, "Can it be poofy?"

Poofy.

I still couldn't name her.

She told me about her foster homes. At first I thought she was slow because she would only give me strange details. My room was blue. We ate mostly macaroni. I was their third foster child. But then she told me about her foster daddy . . .

"Now I get to be at a group home." Her story reminded me of Ollie.

No pity in her voice, just this is what life is.

She said she wanted M&M's. "But no peanuts. I'm allergic."

I bought her a pack and we went to the food court. She poured them on a napkin . . . and ate each one slowly, like they had a secret.

The whole time . . . find a name, come on, Nance, find a name—

Then she took the purple one and rubbed it on her lips.

She looked at me, her lips a bright violet, and said, "Like lipstick. You ever do this?"

Her face was . . .

> *She shakes it off.*

"Do you want to put some on too?" She handed me a red one.

The goodie, the poofy, the purple, but still no name. I took the red one and licked it.

> *She brings the pill up to her lips and licks it. Then takes it away.*

Then she started talking about everything. How she met Sikes. Online. He was really funny and nice; he told her to go to a group home and then maybe she could come live with him. He promised to teach her how to ride a bike.

"Can I come home with you?"

Home. My phone beeped.

"Who's that? Your boyfriend?"

"No . . . he's my . . . he's my . . . I don't know what he is."

Then she stared straight at me. I couldn't breathe. She searched my face. Her face . . . "You look good." What? She pointed at my—

NANCY touches her lips.

"The red looks good."

NANCY whispers to herself and Rose:

I'd do anything for you.

I grabbed her hand. "I'm going to take you to the heart of Toronto. I want you to wait there for a nice man. His name is Oliver. He's strong looking but not tough. He has brown eyes and he knows how to smile just with them. He looks like he could be your . . . half-brother. He's going to take you somewhere nice."

We walked outside into the sour smell of Toronto. Things that shouldn't be mixed, glitter, graffiti, guts. I took her into the middle of Dundas Square. The only part of this city that makes sense— concrete and pretend.

I took my jacket off, put it on her, and said, "Goodbye, Rose."

Sikes

She ready?

The text goes into NANCY. Her body changes and she hurriedly texts him back.

Yes Baby!!!!!

Sikes's rule: Never check in late.

She texts OLIVER.

Nancy

She's waiting for you.
I told her you would be there.
We can protect her. She's different.
Please.
If you do this we leave
today.
I promise. She's a new beginning.
We can have a new beginning.

OLIVER *reads all the texts on his phone.*

OLIVER
And the faucets,
Go and open,
As she pleads with me.

And truth be told,
She's never asked of me.
This rock that never had dew,
Is now crying with me.
Emotions that she swore,
She'd never let the world see.
Now the display of this emotion,
She's entrusting to me.
And if actions trump words,

Like Dodger spit it,
Then the notion of bottom girl,
She's
Counterfeited.

(Ain't that all you really need)
And that's all I really need.

Been wrong about a lot of things,
But I'm right about her.
As reckless as the calling,
I gotta do right by her.
Seventeen years I've been waiting,
For something to fight for.

    NANCY's phone rings; she picks up quickly.

. . . Hey

NANCY
. . . Hey.

OLIVER
Just let me know the details.

NANCY
She's waiting at Dundas Square.

OLIVER
How am I going to find her?

NANCY
She's wearing my jacket. Do this, we go.

OLIVER
Where we going? Disneyland?

NANCY
I don't know. Away from here.

OLIVER
That's what I want.

NANCY
Find a place for her.

>   *Beat.*

I'll find a place for us.

OLIVER
If you serious about leaving, I'll get it done. The shit is going to hit the fan.

NANCY
I'm ready.

OLIVER
Hey.

NANCY
Hey.

>   *NANCY hangs up with relief and then, with sudden panic, she takes her pills and hides them. She texts Dodger, her dealer.*

> Hey Dodge! Going on super soon! Need cotton.
> Double. THANKS!!!

My rule: Never take the last two of anything till the last two minutes.

OLIVER texts Dodger.

Oliver

> D, Backseat action lined up. I need the car
> last year.

Dodger

> Cool. Make sure she a 4 or betta. Come grab
> the keys

OLIVER
Left Dodger under the impression
That I'd moved on.
He knew I had to dip in another's water,
To be certain.
So the young breezy,
From around the way,
That was often flirtin.
The mention of her name,
Became my pawn.

I made a move for a dap,
But he pulled me in for a hug.
And whispered in my ear,
"You've made the right decision."

With the,
Keys to the veeks
In the palm of my hand,
He had that big brother grin.

"The back seat's all you need,
Just make sure and keep it clean,
Wet wipes in the glove compartment,
With some Magnums,
If that's how you packin."

With my deceit buried,
I was his grin's reflection.
That was the Polaroid,
With which I left him.

Now the engine's still humming,
Although I've parked.
And the last specks of rays
Giving way to the dark.

But the Square got so many bodies,
You'd swear they had no home.
Half the city must be suffering
An economic downturn.
But that thought's shot down,
Gucci, Fendi, Prada
Criss-cross one another.

Now where could she be.
And who could she be.
I'm looking for eyes
That's looking for me.
Body frames that ain't yet reach

Age fifteen.
I applied that filter,
But it wasn't helping things.

Nance said she packaged her,
White/bubble/wrap.
But
Was I looking for,
Suitcases or backpacks?
Ripped cardboard with my name,
Weighing down some fragile neck?

Pause.

How ap-ro-pos.
She was in the glow of the Hard Rock Cafe.
Oversized jacket fitting like,
The fur on a celebrity.
Autobiography waiting to be writ,
Hard drugs and alcohol,
Tortured soul,
Slit wrists.

But if she stood,
She'd only stand about ye.
Carnival guess,
She was no more than twelve.
Just a minor niner,
Too eager to graduate.
To adulthood.
And with her home situation,
Being what it is,
She'd probably pinky swear,
That she already did.

With
Just a big smile,
And a couple of lines,
She was hooked and sinkered,
Reeled her in and told her
We'd be taking a ride.

Skyline saying bye-bye.
Street lights had a greater divide.
I could sense she was squirming,
Uncomfortable in her seat.
Luckily
We were where the,
Yellow brick road and the asphalt meet.

Geared down
And parked across the street.

The curtains hadn't changed
In the years gone by.
And Big Bird was still pushing
That same red whip (car).
Still no man in her life,
Or if there was,
He wasn't handy,
Porch light still shorting.

Searched my soul,
For the pastor,
As she put her hand,
On my clutch hand.
Before the sermon could begin,
I took my other hand and sandwiched hers in.

"Rose,
My name is Oliver.
I'm not your pimp.
What we in the midst of doing,
Could get me kilt.

I know how dark it is,
That place you coming from.
Where pain is just a secret,
You can't share with no one.

But where you running to won't help you none.
Family, out there,
Is just an abstract notion.

If it wasn't me in this car,
You coulda been raped or kilt,
Introduced to a life of knee-highs
Raped and kilt.

Not going to tell you
That you shouldn'ta ran.
I got shin splints to testify
I did a few miles myself.

What you searching for,
Is a safe haven.
And that cavalcade of lights
Had you drawn in.
But it's three-card Monte,
Ole bait and switch.
You gonna find it too hot,
You gonna find it too cold,
Goldilocks.

Just right,
Ain't words those streets hold.

Now the woman in this
Safe house,
She won't harm you.
You won't be forced to do nothing
You don't wanna do.
She's just extra time,
So you can think things through."

Youngin was a little hesitant at first,
But the Fahrenheit of my smile,
Drew her outside.

They say white women age,
But Big Bird looked the same.
Attention to detail,
Her image itched in my brain.

Not close enough to hug her,
But we were hugging from a distance.
Head on her chest,
From a distance.
"Don't cry, it's okay.
You did nothing wrong."
From a distance.
That was the space,
Wherein
We did our healing.

I took off Nance's protective armour,
White/bubble/wrap.
Bird

Put her arms around her.
Like
For
Like.
And the drop-off was done.

Bird, I need you to make a call for me.

(aside) Some plans are conjured in haste.

    OLIVER texts NANCY.

Oliver

It's done.

Nancy

How long till you get here?

Soon! Driving back into city.

    NANCY pauses, then texts Dodger.

Nancy

U COMING????

Dodger

Held up. u cool?

On in 2 not feeling up to it!!!!!!!!!

K. junkie.

    NANCY texts OLIVER.

Nancy

Text when you're close, may need a bit
more time.

> Why?

Tying up some loose ends.

> What type of ends???
> I did my part. don't flake out on me.

No flaking just may need a little more time x.

> This is the bullshit I hate. Nance don't let the hillbilly heron take us down.

TRUST ME.

> get your shit. Then we gone.

My Nance got that itch
That you can't scratch.
Cocaine fingernail can't reach
That dig a hole to fill a hole.
Flawed remedy.
Ninety-five billion sold.

But they all hungry.
Consumption by the consumed.
Welcome to the jungle
It ain't no Nirvana.
Is all drugs and no roses,
And the hollow souls it harbours.
Singing,
My baaaby,
I'll make you feel good,
I'll make you feel good,
My baaaby
'S got that itch that you can't scratch.

NANCY sits, searching the Internet for maps. Her porn site gets an online request. She types. "Try me later!" NANCY touches her bare arms.

NANCY
I miss my jacket.

Nancy
Eta?????

Dodger
IDK

Oliver
You figure out where we're going?

Nancy
Yes.

You got a map?

NANCY is shaking. Her wrists aching, she wrings them out. She goes back to her computer.

You can find anything on the Internet. When I was little I was addicted to the glow. I could never sleep. There was this feeling, at the pit of me. It'd keep me up real late staring at the screen. I'd look up maps online. I was obsessed with finding the distance between things.

She looks at a series of real maps and fantasy maps. Oz, Narnia, Middle Earth.

No, no. No.

She pulls up a full-colour map of Neverland.

Maybe.

She thinks about it a bit, then moves on to another map. Of Niagara the city. She clicks on various pictures, carefully avoiding pictures of the falls.

Finally, on my twelfth birthday, my parents agreed to take me to Niagara. But Mom got anxious packing the car. She fell apart over the SNACKS. It was the only time I threw a tantrum. I started screaming and crying.

She whispers.

Please don't take this moment from me.

Still holding her rib she texts OLIVER.

Nancy

You got a passport? We're going Southside. xx

NANCY goes to where she put her last two pills. She stands in front of them, willing herself not to take one. She texts Dodger instead.

Nancy

Dodge, get here NOW!!!!

so my dad took me to Niagara. We're driving in and the first thing I see is this maze with a picture of a family all doing this— *(does the expression of mock surprise)* And I say I want to go in. So, he drops me off and says he's going to run some errands.

She digs her fingers into her rib.

I got lost. In a kids' maze. You had to collect some bullshit sword and find three towers. I found two towers and a sword but I couldn't find the third tower. I couldn't get out. I looked for hours, around and around.

NANCY picks up one pill.

And then, deep in the maze, I felt something so pure.

I want more.

I turned this plastic purple corner and this thing just dropped in me.

I want more.

She plays with the pill, turning it over in her hands.

The first time I got high I thought, oh, so this is the point of life. Why the hell didn't anyone tell me sooner?

She holds the pill up.

Please, sir, I want some more.

She takes it. Lights shift to OLIVER.

OLIVER picks up his phone and makes a call to Big Bird, his former foster mom.

OLIVER
Hey, Birdie, how's Rose doing? Thanks for taking her in. Did you make that call for me? . . . You told the cops about Sikes . . . They picked him up already? . . .

OLIVER nods.

Good. Good. I owe you. Thanks.

OLIVER hangs up.

Maybe it's more hate than morals. I hate the fact that Sikes still means something to her.

Hate that the weakest parts of her are because of him. Either way, she'll thank me for it.

Lights shift to NANCY.

NANCY
Years later I learned there's a way to get out of a maze. Any maze. If you take your hand and put it on the side of the wall and you walk touching every corner the whole way through, never taking your hand off, you're guaranteed to make it out. It's called the wall follower.

NANCY's high settles in. Her shoulders ease up.

I've always wanted to go back to that shitty kids' maze and try it out. Get to that last tower. Get my moment of— *(does the mock surprise expression)*

NANCY's phone rings. She picks it up.

You close? What . . . Calm down . . . I can't hear you. WHAT? What happened to him? Start again, the police came . . . NO—I did what I was supposed to do: I dropped her off at the front door like I always do—I did—cross my heart . . . No. No, baby. No. Why would I ever do that? Baby—I would never do that to

Sikes—you know that—I would never do that to my man, to you, to the family. You'll fix it. Won't you? You're still coming, right? You're still bringing my—Dodger? Listen, you're still bringing—No—please.

PLEASE.

FUCK.

NANCY, panicked, calls OLIVER.

What did you do?

OLIVER
What?

NANCY
Sikes got picked up by the police. Please tell me you weren't involved.

OLIVER
You're pissed he got picked up? Are you shittin me?

NANCY
We had a plan to leave. Not do this.

OLIVER
You. Are. Sick. I put my life on the line. Screw you. You're all lies. You said you were ready.

NANCY
Dodger is freaking out. He thinks I was involved and Sikes, he thinks . . . Oh god—it's a mess now. All I wanted was for you to get her safe and us to go. This is a mess—

OLIVER

Nothing is a mess. I'm grabbing you and we leave. Stop freaking out like a damn druggie.

NANCY

You have no idea what you've done. He's coming for me. He's—

OLIVER

I'm coming for you. I'm going to get you out of there.

NANCY

I have to fix this.

OLIVER

What?

NANCY

He needs me.

OLIVER

That shit you on got you delusional. You fail me.

NANCY

FUCK YOU.

OLIVER

All you women do is fail me.

NANCY

You're right. I was never going to leave. It's all fucking lies. I'm going to stay here and fuck Sikes—

> OLIVER *hangs up on her.*

> Yo! Answer your damn phone. Need the car. Yur girly did some shifty shit.

NANCY is shaking. She takes her last pill. Another request comes on for a live cam show.

Please, sir, can I want some more.

She touches her chest, her wrist, and her thigh.

Pain in my chest. Sadness in my wrist. Whisper in my thigh.

NANCY's high settles in as she prepares herself for her last live cam show.

Beat. She digs her fingers into her ribs with her eyes closed.

She opens her eyes suddenly and stares out.

As she speaks she begins to do a dance/strip show for the webcam. But it's a peculiar dance done to her own rhythm

I make a lot of bad decisions, but I understand words.

Sikes makes me feel special. Problem is you have to not feel special most of the time for that to work.

OLIVER
I shoulda listened to Dodger that first time.

NANCY

I'm not some young girl no one misses. ScarboroughKitty, Tinyxx, everbe, lookinsee2004, nope that's not me. Sikes misses me. Misses me, never sees me. It's all in how you tell it.

She dances loose and high. It is not a sexy dance. It is a private, childlike dance to herself.

OLIVER

You are who he said you was.

NANCY

I fell in love with Sikes because he gave me my freedom. Problem is. Now, my freedom comes in the shape of something that always runs out. I work for my hit. I'm a proxy for my oxy.

She smiles, pleased with that, then drops it immediately.

OLIVER

I should have listened.

NANCY

Sikes was my first love. He created me. Problem is. Second love changes you.

OLIVER

Dodger was
Disgusted at me,
Morphed to pity.

NANCY

Problem is . . .

OLIVER
I was convincing myself
The fuel was envy.

NANCY
When I get high the sky opens up, there's a small tear in the heavens. Problem is, the tear stretched and now all of heaven's leaking out.

OLIVER
All I did was mention her name.

NANCY
I'm covered in heaven.

OLIVER
And what I'd do to her man,
And how come you never shot the sheriff,
After her mistreatment.

NANCY
You can dress a story different.

OLIVER
" 'Cause I'm his deputy,
And past what you understand
She still considers him her man!"

NANCY
But does it change its expression?

OLIVER
"I shoulda never brought you
So close."

NANCY
First time my rib hit the bedpost.

OLIVER
"Put your face in it,
Tongue could taste the temptation."

Dodger shook his head.

NANCY
Second time hurt.

OLIVER
"You don't wanna be that young boy
Covered in lead,
Tryna make a housewife
Outta one
Whose already made her bed."

NANCY
Third time Sikes broke my rib on his body.

OLIVER
"Musta been lost in translation."

NANCY
Sikes asked me.

OLIVER
"Between all that texting."

NANCY
"Do you know who you are, and what you are?"

OLIVER
"But I seen it all replayed."

NANCY
"Oh, yes, I know all about it."

OLIVER
"At the end of the day—"

NANCY
"I've brought many girls into hell."

OLIVER
"Actions trump words.
She'll show
She's his bottom girl!"

NANCY
It's like anything else.

OLIVER
And with those shots fired—

NANCY
White pill.

OLIVER
He left me handicapped.

NANCY
Yum.

OLIVER
With no words
To put out there.
No words to retract.

NANCY
You can convince yourself of anything.

OLIVER
I just never saw
Homegirl like that.

NANCY
I love Sikes.

OLIVER
But he said—

NANCY
Won't say I don't.

OLIVER
That was his bottom girl.

NANCY
But love is a word
Like—

OLIVER
(more melodic) Sikes's bottom girl.
His bottom bottom girl.

NANCY
Like—

OLIVER
Knees on the floor.
Hands spread
apart.

NANCY
Like—

OLIVER
Nervous beating of the little girl heart.
That's his bottom girl.

NANCY
I'm good with words.

OLIVER
You know the first cut.

NANCY
Remember?

OLIVER
Is the deepest, deepest—

NANCY
I'm elastic.

OLIVER
And when she bleeds—

NANCY
It's all how I tell it.

OLIVER
The first scar—

NANCY
Save the best for last.

OLIVER
Runs the deepest, deepest.

NANCY
You know the story.

OLIVER
That's his bottom girl.

NANCY
I'm the girl who's stuck.

OLIVER
It's a slow heal
For the bottom girl.

NANCY
You're the boy who's afraid.

OLIVER
Thighs spread apart,
He ready to pounce.
He don't want the fruit ripe.

NANCY
I—

OLIVER
He want the fruit young.

NANCY
Wanted.

OLIVER
That's his bottom girl.
Get it—

NANCY
A sniff.

OLIVER
—before—

NANCY
A hit.

OLIVER
—the sun.

NANCY
A jacket.

OLIVER
His bottom girl.

NANCY
I know the story.

OLIVER
Still she believes.

NANCY
But still I believe.

OLIVER
In deliverance from the wood.

NANCY
In magic.

OLIVER
The makings of a bottom girl.

NANCY
I'm—

OLIVER
Arch in her back.

NANCY
I'm—

OLIVER
With his elbow in her spine.

NANCY
I'm—

OLIVER
And the other hand grip up.

NANCY
Looking—

OLIVER
As he takes she from behind.

NANCY
Looking—

OLIVER
With her bottom in the air.

NANCY
Looking / looking—

OLIVER
And if she cries,
He wont hear.

NANCY
—for—

OLIVER
He—

NANCY
—my—

OLIVER
—just—

NANCY
—my—

OLIVER
Beat it up
Beat it up

Beat it up.
Wood in ah she—

NANCY
—my / my—

OLIVER
Rip it up
Rip it up
Rip it up.

NANCY
My map.

OLIVER
When he done
She'll feel bruised,
But won't call it abuse.
Somehow she'll find love
In this scar tissue.

> *NANCY* **stares** *at OLIVER.*

NANCY
It's you.

OLIVER
His bottom girl.

NANCY
No.

OLIVER
You're his bottom girl.

NANCY
No.

OLIVER
You're his bottom bottom girl.

NANCY
No.
I found. My map.
In you.

> *With this realization* NANCY *grabs her phone.*

Nancy
I'm ready to leave this life. Come get me now.

OLIVER
But a phoenix
Don't stay on the ground.

NANCY
This is the moment.

OLIVER
You must rise
And rise and rise to the sun.

> NANCY *reads her text aloud:*

Nancy
I'm glad you fucked Sikes.

This one they must have gotten wrong.
Fuck what they hearrrd,
You're more than a bottom girl.

NANCY

Do you think you could use your hand to find your way out of life? If you touch every corner always, will it let you free?

OLIVER

What's her ritual of preparation?
Maybe she's like Big Bird,
Cut from that same cloth.
Has she been sitting on the toilet,
Her leg stretched out to the tub,
Lathered up, razor in hand.
My memory of this involves cotton towels
Wrapped around the chest.
But if she is alone,
Maybe alone equates to undressed.
Is she smiling,
Is she singing,
Is she thinking
While she's shavin?
Is you smiling, singing, thinking, of . . .
Maybe she traces the inside of her thighs with her favourite perfume.
A dab behind each ear.
A high-wire crossing of her collarbone . . .
Caught up in the rapture
Of what ifs.

She changes the image on her screen to a picture of Niagara Falls. Powerful, expansive, and beautiful. NANCY hurries, grabbing a few things to put in her bag.

The ding of her phone.

NANCY remains perfectly still. She approaches her phone carefully. She looks down at it.

Dodger
You're fucking dead.

She freezes. Then closes her eyes and whispers.

NANCY
I must have gone too far to turn back.

She opens her eyes and texts OLIVER quickly.

Nancy
Wait in the parking lot for me.

Oliver
Nah, I'm almost here. I'll come get you.

No. I want to come to you. It's important to me. PLEASE.

There's a sound outside her door. OLIVER arrives in the parking lot holding the bubble jacket, the space we first saw him in.

Nancy
I want to leave from where we first met.

OLIVER stops and waits.

There's a knock at NANCY's *door.*

The picture of the falls comes alive. The water pours.

Oliver

`K. be quick.`

Nancy

NANCY speaks as she writes.

Stuck. Afraid.

The knock turns to pounding. NANCY *hurriedly types on her phone. The walls shake. The water of the falls comes down with great force.* NANCY *continues typing on her phone.*

Her room shakes from the knocking. NANCY *sends her last text. She approaches the door and looks out to the audience.*

Rose looks like him. I can't explain it. She looks like me too.

She opens the door. Blackout in her space.

OLIVER
These seconds can't help but be minutes.
These minutes will be hours.
I can't wait any longer.

OLIVER holds NANCY's *bubble jacket in his hand. He begins to walk towards* NANCY's *apartment.*

So this is what I'm forced to do to see her.
To see her
Each nostril locks its door.
To see her
Nerves steady their reign.
To see her
My steps outpace their past.

We hear NANCY *hiccupping. The hiccupping starts to turn to choking.*

And
I'm there before I know it.
Pinching my skin,
Come on, pores, exude it.
Standing there
Like I figured I'd do on prom night.
Momma and Poppa apprehension.
Arms and legs starched out.
But the feeling is fading,
As I envision her at five, four, three—
Whatever on the other side of that door—
Two, one—
Fearless.

The choking stops. Silence.

OLIVER'*s phone dings with a text.*

Dodger

She didn't name you. Get your foot on the gas, don't ever come back.
Caged bird won't be singing now.

OLIVER looks down at the texts.

Fearless.

> *He opens the door to* NANCY's *apartment.* OLIVER *is suspended in time.*

> *The world shifts again.*

> *Texts come flying back in. We see the entirety of the relationship, starting with* HEY . . . *and ending with one last long text we haven't seen from* NANCY *yet.*

> *Lights shift to the opening state, back to the parking lot where we first saw* OLIVER. *The sun has just come up revealing the morning.*

That night I felt like I let you down. 'Cause I wanted to save you . . . *(looks at phone)* but the whole time you were saving me.

> *He scrolls to* NANCY's *final text.*

You were trying to save me with these words.

> OLIVER *looks down at the last thing written to him by* NANCY.

Wait for it.

> NANCY's *last text appears.*

> OLIVER *reads it aloud:*

Nancy

> I'm the girl who was stuck to a freezing pole for three hours.
> You're the boy who's scared of hot dogs.
> I'm the girl who needs something always.
> Something to make her warm.
> A hit. A sniff. A jacket.
> You're the boy who's been searching for a home.
> Place to place, fear to fear, story to story.
> I gave her my jacket because I don't need mine now.
> You gave her a home because you're not searching anymore.
> This is the moment.

This is the moment.

I wish you never said "elephant shoe." I never said "olive juice." We never said "Hey" . . . I wish just one time . . .

I love you.

> OLIVER *gets up and faces the audience.*

Two things you should know before we end.

ONE: Some people fear death.
My biggest fear was that I was already dead.
If life be love and love be safe.

TWO: Nancy was the realest thing I ever knew.

> *Blackout.*

A Dickens text comes up:

Charles

> There are books of which the backs and covers are by far the best parts—Oliver Twist.

ACKNOWLEDGEMENTS

Factory Theatre, b current, Obsidian Theatre Company, Nina Lee Aquino, Nigel Shawn Williams, Philip Akin, Jajube Mandiela, Jonathan Heppner, Renna Reddie, Susanna Fournier, Ngabo Nabea, and our beloved and brilliant dramaturge, Iris Turcott.

Twisted received funding from the Ontario Arts Council.

Charlotte Corbeil-Coleman is a multiple-award-winning play-wright. She graduated from the playwriting program at the National Theatre School of Canada and has gone on to write for theatre, radio, film, and television. Selected writing credits include *The End of Pretending*; *Scratch*, which was nominated for a Dora Mavor Moore Award and a Governor General's Literary Award; and CBC Radio's *Afghanada*. Most recently she has been working on three feature films. Charlotte lives in Toronto.

Joseph Jomo Pierre was born in Trinidad and raised in Scarborough, Canada, where he completed a BFA in acting at York University. He is the author of *Shakespeare's Nigga*, a finalist for the Governor General's Literary Award for Drama, as well as *BeatDown: Three Plays*, which includes *Born Ready*, *BeatDown*, and *Pusha-Man*. He lives in Toronto.

First edition: June 2017
Printed and bound in Canada by Marquis Book Printing, Montreal

Cover illustration and design by Patrick Gray

PLAYWRIGHTS
CANADA PRESS

202-269 Richmond St. W.
Toronto, ON
M5V 1X1

416.703.0013
info@playwrightscanada.com
www.playwrightscanada.com
@playcanpress

RECYCLED
Paper made from
recycled material
FSC® C103567

Printed on Rolland Enviro, which contains 100% post-
consumer fiber, is ECOLOGO, Processed Chlorine Free,
Ancient Forest Friendly and FSC® certified
and is manufactured using renewable biogas energy.

PERMANENT   100%   BIO GAS   Ancient Forest Friendly™